Management Accounting: Costing Wise Guide

AAT Advanced Diploma in Accounting

© Aubrey Penning, 2016. Reprinted 2017.

Image of owl © Eric Isselée-Fotolia.com

Published by Osborne Books Limited
Tel 01905 748071, Email books@osbornebooks.co.uk, Website ww'

Printed and bound by Stroma Ltd, UK.

ISBN 978 1911198 055

how to use this Wise Guide

This Wise Guide has been designed to supplement your Tutorial and Workbook. It has two main aims:

- ▓ to reinforce your learning as you study your course
- ▓ to help you prepare for your online assessment

This Wise Guide is organised in the specific topic areas listed on pages 4 and 5. These individual topic areas have been designed to cover the main areas of study, concentrating on specific areas of difficulty. There is also an index at the back to help you find the areas you are studying or revising.

The Owl symbolises wisdom, and acts as your tutor, introducing and explaining topics. Please let us know if he is doing his job properly. If you have feedback on this material please email books@osbornebooks.co.uk

Thank you and good luck with your study and revision.

Osborne Books

REVISION TIPS

*'OWL' stands for: **O**bserve **W**rite **L**earn*

There are a number of well-known ways in which you can remember information:

- *You can remember what it looks like on the page. Diagrams, lists, mind-maps, colour coding for different types of information, all help you **observe** and remember.*

- *You can remember what you **write** down. Flash cards, post-it notes around the bathroom mirror, notes on a mobile phone all help. It is the process of writing which fixes the information in the brain.*

- *You can **learn** by using this Wise Guide. Read through each topic carefully and then prepare your own written version on flash cards, post-it notes, wall charts – anything that you can see regularly.*

- *Lastly, give yourself **chill out** time, your brain a chance to recover and the information time to sink in. Promise yourself treats when you have finished studying – a drink, chocolate, a work out. Relax! And pass.*

list of contents

1 Costing

INTRODUCTION

This unit involves examining the costs that are incurred in organisations. It also describes the revenue (or income) that is generated and explains how decisions that affect profit (revenue minus costs) can be made.

why carry out costing?

This part of management accounting helps managers to:

■ record, monitor and control costs

■ plan for the future

■ make decisions for

  – the short term, and

  – the long term

how does cost accounting differ from financial accounting?

This unit concentrates on cost accounting, as seen in the following diagram.

All accounting must be carried out with integrity.

	FINANCIAL ACCOUNTING	COST ACCOUNTING
Data used:	Financial transactions	Financial transactions and external information, eg inflation rates
Formats:	Financial Statements: profit or loss, financial position	Management reports
Focus:	Past events	Future planning
Purpose:	Assess financial performance	Assist decision-making, planning and control
Produced:	At the end of a financial period	During a financial period
Users:	External: shareholders, banks	Internal: by management

2 Classifying costs

WAYS TO CLASSIFY COSTS

There are four main ways that costs can be classified (divided up). Although at first this classification process can seem confusing, each method is logical and needs to be understood.

classification by element

There are three elements of cost as follows:

- **materials** – the physical stuff that is used to make things or provide services (eg rubber used to make tyres or detergent to clean windows)

- **labour** – the cost of employing people to do things (eg a machine operator or a salesperson)

- **expenses** – costs which are neither materials nor labour (eg rent or electricity)

classification by nature

The meaning of this term is not immediately obvious. It means dividing costs into **direct** costs and **indirect** costs.

▨ **direct costs** are costs that can be identified directly with each unit of output – these costs can be traced straight to the things being made or the service being provided. Units of output are also known as 'cost units'.

Examples of direct costs include:

- the costs of materials used to make products
- the cost of paying the people who are 'hands on' and directly involved in the manufacture of a product

▨ **indirect costs** are the other costs – those that cannot be identified directly with each unit of output. These are often costs incurred in order to help make various products or provide a range of services.

Examples of indirect costs include:

- the cost of factory supervisors
- the cost of insurance

Indirect costs are also known as **overheads**.

classification by function

Costs can also be classified according to the **function** of the part of the organisation, eg the department that incurs the cost.

The main functions normally used for classification are:

- **production**

- **administration**

- **selling and distribution**

- **finance**

a note on function names:

- the function names are often the same as the department names

- 'production costs' may be referred to as 'factory costs'

- the administration, selling and distribution and finance costs may be referred to as 'warehouse' or 'office' costs

classification by behaviour

The idea of 'cost behaviour' refers to what happens to the total of any cost when the level of output changes.

The main types of **cost behaviour** are:

- **fixed costs** – these do not change in total when output changes
  Example: the cost of rent does not increase when output increases

- **variable costs** – the total amount of a variable cost changes in proportion to the level of output
  Example: the total cost of materials increases as output increases

- **semi-variable costs** – these are a combination of fixed and variable costs
  Example: the cost of electricity that includes a standing charge and a usage charge

- **stepped fixed costs** – these costs are fixed within a range of output, but then 'step' up to a higher level for output in a higher range
  Example: an additional supervisor is required when output increases above a certain level

WHAT ARE RESPONSIBILITY CENTRES?

These are used to enable managers to control the parts of the business for which they are responsible.

There are three types of responsibility centre. Each type is defined by what the centre does and what the manager can control.

types of responsibility centre

Responsibility centres are parts of the organisation where a particular manager has control. They may be parts of the functions of the business.

The types are:

▓ **cost centres** – where the manager just controls costs

Example: an 'assembly' cost centre within the production function

■ **profit centres** – where the manager is responsible for both the revenues and the costs that result in profit

Example: the 'used cars' section of a car dealership; here the manager will be responsible for both buying and selling the used cars

■ **investment centres** – where the manager is accountable for the profit compared to the amount invested

Example: a single shop within a chain of shops; here the shop manager is responsible for making a profit and this is compared with the total investment in net assets in that shop

■ **revenue centres** – where the manager is accountable for the revenue from sales

Example: an organisation that sells products into geographical regions; here each sales manager is responsible for the sales in his region

Responsibility centres can be used in conjunction with cost classification to analyse costs within cost accounting systems.

The cost for each 'cost unit' can then ultimately be calculated.

4 Managing materials inventory

WHY CONTROL INVENTORY LEVELS?

Organisations should make sure that they hold an appropriate level of inventory of the various materials that they need.

If they hold too much inventory they risk storage and cash flow problems; too little and they may run out of inventory and bring production to a halt.

useful terminology

We need to understand the following terms so that we can use various methods to control the level of inventories:

- **inventory buffer** – the extra amount of inventory that is held as a contingency (a 'reserve') – in case things do not go according to plan and there is the danger that inventory may run out

- **lead time** – the length of time between placing an order for more material and it actually arriving

- **re-order level** – when the inventory level drops to the re-order level it is time to place an order for more material

- **re-order quantity** – the quantity of material that should be ordered each time (do not confuse this with the re-order level!)

- **maximum inventory level** – the largest amount of a material that will be held at any one time (it may be based on the capacity of the warehouse) – this will occur just after a delivery arrives

These terms are shown in the diagram below and their calculation on the pages that follow.

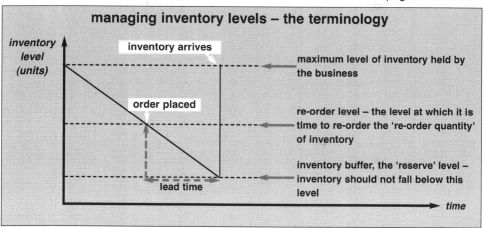

inventory calculations

■ **re-order level** is the level of inventory units held when it will be necessary to re-order so that the inventory delivered will arrive well before the inventory runs out; the calculation is based on daily usage, the lead time and the 'buffer' level:

= (average usage x average lead time) + inventory buffer

■ **maximum inventory level** is reached when a new delivery has just arrived; if this was ordered when the inventory had reached the re-order level it should arrive when the inventory reaches the 'buffer' point – the maximum inventory level is:

= inventory buffer + maximum re-order quantity

■ **re-order quantity** is decided by management as follows:

– the **minimum re-order quantity** will be just enough to avoid the inventory level going below the inventory buffer:

= average usage x average lead time

– the **maximum re-order quantity** will avoid the inventory level going over the maximum inventory level:

= maximum inventory level – inventory buffer

economic order quantity (EOQ)

This is the optimum (most economic) amount to order – to calculate it we need to know the following:

- **annual usage** – how many units are used each year (eg 20,000 units)

- **ordering cost** – the amount it costs to place one order (the administration cost), £50 for example

- **inventory holding cost** – the cost of keeping one unit for one year (based on warehousing, insurance etc) (eg £2)

With this information we can calculate the EOQ as follows:

$EOQ = \sqrt{(2 \text{ x annual usage x ordering cost}) \div \text{inventory holding cost}}$

Using the example figures quoted above this gives:

$EOQ = \sqrt{(2 \text{ x } 20{,}000 \text{ x £50}) \div £2}$

$= \sqrt{1{,}000{,}000}$

$= 1{,}000 \text{ units}$

5 Inventory valuation

HOW TO CALCULATE 'COST'

The 'cost' of the materials used and the inventory remaining will depend on the valuation method that is used.

There are three methods that we need to understand and use for calculations. Two are based on the notional order in which inventory is used: (FIFO and LIFO) and the other (AVCO) is based on an average cost.

outline of the three methods

- **First In First Out (FIFO)** assumes that **the materials that arrive first are used first,** and so the valuation of the first issue of inventory is based on the cost of the first delivery. This means that it is possible that issues and balances of inventory at any one time can be split for valuation purposes and based on more than one price.

- **Last In First Out (LIFO)** assumes the opposite – that **the latest deliveries are used first** and the valuation of each issue of inventory is based on the cost of the latest delivery and not the first delivery. This can also result in split valuations.

- **Weighted Average Cost (AVCO)** is different from FIFO and LIFO – it does not assume any particular order of usage, but works out **an average cost based on all the deliveries**.

  A weighted average cost (AVCO) is calculated each time more inventory arrives and this cost is used for both issues and balances until the next delivery arrives and the average is re-calculated.

You may well have studied Costing in the previous level of your course and you should already be familiar with the way in which FIFO, LIFO and AVCO work.

Note:

- The actual order in which inventory is used does not have any impact on the choice of valuation methods.

- LIFO cannot be used for valuations in financial statements, but the method is still acceptable for internal management accounting purposes within an organisation.

  When inventory valuations are used for financial accounting purposes, FIFO or AVCO can be used consistently to determine inventory 'cost'. The inventory value to include in the financial statements is then determined by comparing this cost figure with 'net realisable value' and the lower figure is used.

EXAMPLE – inventory valuation using FIFO

Inventory – Widgets (Medium)								
Date	**Receipts**			**Issues**			**Balance**		
	Qty	Cost Each £	Total Cost £	Qty	Cost Each £	Total Cost £	Qty	Cost Each £	Total Cost £
1 Nov							100	2.00	200
2 Nov	400	2.10	840				100 <u>400</u> 500	2.00 2.10	200 <u>840</u> 1,040
3 Nov				100 <u>150</u> 250	2.00 2.10	200 <u>315</u> 515	250	2.10	525
14 Nov	450	2.30	1,035				250 <u>450</u> 700	2.10 2.30	525 <u>1,035</u> 1,560
15 Nov				250 <u>250</u> 500	2.10 2.30	525 <u>575</u> 1,100	200	2.30	460

The calculations in this example are explained below.

EXAMPLE – inventory valuation using FIFO explained

The cost of **the issue of 250 units on 3 Nov** is worked out as follows:

100 units are matched with the opening balance of 100 units at £2.00 each	£200
150 units are matched with part of the receipt on 2 Nov at £2.10 each	£315
Total cost of issue	£515

This leaves the balance on 3 Nov matched with the remainder of the receipt on 2 Nov and valued at 250 x £2.10 = £525.

The cost of **the issue of 500 units on 15 Nov** is worked out as follows:

250 units are matched with the rest of the receipt on 2 Nov at £2.10 each	£525
250 units are matched with part of the receipt on 14 Nov at £2.30 each	£575
Total cost of issue	£1,100

This leaves the balance on 15 Nov matched with the remainder of the receipt on 14 Nov and valued at 200 x £2.30 = £460.

*Note that in an assessment you may need to carry out the calculations of the split valuations outside the table and only insert the **total** units and **total** cost for both issues and balances in the spaces provided.*

EXAMPLE – inventory valuation using LIFO

Inventory – Widgets (Medium)								
Date	Receipts			Issues			Balance		
	Qty	Cost Each £	Total Cost £	Qty	Cost Each £	Total Cost £	Qty	Cost Each £	Total Cost £
1 Nov							100	2.00	200
2 Nov	400	2.10	840				100	2.00	200
							400	2.10	840
							500		1,040
3 Nov				250	2.10	525	100	2.00	200
							150	2.10	315
							250		515
14 Nov	450	2.30	1,035				100	2.00	200
							150	2.10	315
							450	2.30	1,035
							700		1,550
15 Nov				450	2.30	1,035	100	2.00	200
				50	2.10	105	100	2.10	210
				500		1,140	200		410

The calculations in this example are explained below.

EXAMPLE – inventory valuation using LIFO explained

The cost of **the issue of 250 units on 3 Nov** is worked out as follows:

All the 250 units are matched with the receipt of 400 units on 2 Nov (the 'last in') at £2.10 each = £525

This leaves the balance on 3 Nov matched with the opening balance plus the 150 units remaining from the receipt on 2 Nov as shown in the table.

The cost of the issue of **500 units on 15 Nov** is worked out as follows:

450 units matched with all of the latest receipt on 14 Nov at £2.30 each	£1,035
50 units matched with part of the earlier receipt on 2 Nov at £2.10 each	£105
Total cost of issue	£1,140

This leaves the **balance on 15 Nov** matched with the following:

The opening balance of 100 units at £2.00	£200
The 100 units remaining from the receipt on 2 Nov valued at £2.10	£210
Cost of balance	£410

EXAMPLE – inventory valuation using AVCO

Inventory – Widgets (Medium)								
Date	Receipts			Issues			Balance		
	Qty	Cost Each £	Total Cost £	Qty	Cost Each £	Total Cost £	Qty	Cost Each £	Total Cost £
1 Nov							100	2.0000	200
2 Nov	400	2.10	840				500	2.0800	1,040
3 Nov				250	2.0800	520	250	2.0800	520
14 Nov	450	2.30	1,035				700	2.2214	1,555
15 Nov				500	2.2214	1,111	200	2.2214	444

The calculations in this example are shown on the next page. Note that the above example uses calculations to 4 decimal places. You will be told in your AAT assessment the number of decimal places that will be required. Note also that for all valuation methods the total (cost of issues + valuation of final balance) is identical. This is an important feature and a useful check on calculations.

EXAMPLE – inventory valuation using AVCO

This method does not use a matching process, but instead calculates an average value per unit after each receipt and then uses that valuation for both issues and balances until the next receipt.

The **average value per unit after the receipt on 2 Nov** is calculated as:

Total cost (£200 opening balance + £840 receipt)	= £1,040
£1,040 divided by total units (100 + 400 = 500)	= £2.0800 per unit

This is used to value both the issue on 3 Nov, and the balance on 3 Nov.

The **average value per unit after the receipt on 14 Nov** is calculated as:

Total cost (£520 previous balance + £1,035 receipt)	= £1,555
£1,555 divided by total units (250 + 450 = 700)	= £2.2214 per unit

This is then used to value the issue and balance on 15 Nov, and also any further issues and balances until a further receipt arrives.

implications of the valuation method used

Because the cost of materials used is a deduction in the calculation of profit, the choice of valuation method will have an impact on recorded profits. Remember:

- if the cost of issues is higher (and the value of remaining inventory therefore lower) the profit will be lower, but . . .

- if the cost of issues is lower (and the value of remaining inventory therefore higher) the profit will be higher

In times of inflation (rising costs) the impact of valuation methods will be as follows:

- **FIFO** will result in higher values for remaining inventory and therefore **higher recorded profits**

- **LIFO** will result in the opposite – lower inventory valuation and **lower recorded profits**

- **AVCO** will result in a recorded profit which is **in between** the other two methods

If there are generally falling prices then the valuation method will of course have the opposite effect to the above. Remember that once an inventory valuation method has been chosen, it must be applied consistently.

inventory valuation – summary

	FIFO	LIFO	AVCO
principles	issues matched with earliest receipts in time order	issues matched with latest receipts in reverse time order	no issue matching – weighted average cost calculated after each receipt
uses	management accounts and financial accounts	management accounts only	management accounts and financial accounts
effects of inflation (rising prices)	higher recorded inventory valuation and higher profits	lower recorded inventory valuation and lower profits	the averaging process will reduce and smooth out the wider variations in inventory valuation and in profit or loss caused by inflation or deflation
effects of deflation (falling prices)	lower recorded inventory valuation and lower profits	higher recorded inventory valuation and higher profits	

6 Labour costs

CALCULATING LABOUR COSTS

In this AAT unit you will need to know how to calculate employee pay. There are three main calculations involved: payment of basic pay, overtime, and bonuses. The actual calculations are quite straightforward, but understanding exactly what is required by the assessment tasks can provide a challenge!

the three types of employee pay

■ **basic rate of pay** is the rate (usually hourly) that is paid for the normal hours of work

■ **overtime** (time in excess of normal working hours) is often paid at a higher rate – this may be expressed in terms of the basic rate (for example 'at time and a half') or as a 'premium' – an extra bit – which is added to the basic rate (for example a premium of £5 per hour is added to a basic rate of £10 per hour to give a total overtime rate of £15 per hour)

■ **bonuses** may be paid for production in excess of a stated level – this can be an individual bonus (for individual performance), or a group bonus that is worked out on the performance of a group and shared between the individuals

---

EXAMPLE – using basic pay and overtime

A company pays its production workers a basic rate of £10 per hour and a premium for any overtime work of £5 per hour. During the first week of November the employees worked 630 hours which included 80 overtime hours.

There are two alternative ways of carrying out the calculation of total pay:

1 Basic hours (550 x £10 = £5,500) + overtime hours (80 x £15 = £1,200)
  Total cost = £6,700

2 Total hours at basic rate (630 x £10 = £6,300) + overtime premium (80 x £5 = £400)
  Total cost = £6,700

The method to be used will depend on the exact requirements of the task – you may need to insert specific figures when you work out the answer.

EXAMPLE – using bonuses

A company pays its production workers a basic rate of £10 per hour and a premium for any overtime work of £5 per hour. A production target is set at 4 units for each labour hour worked (including overtime hours). A group bonus is payable of £1.50 per unit produced in excess of the target. During the first week of November the employees worked 630 hours which included 80 overtime hours. The production level achieved was 2,700 units.

The calculation is shown below on the left and the workings are on the right:

Basic pay (including basic hours for overtime)	£6,300	*(630 x £10)*
+ Overtime premium	£400	*(80 x £5)*
+ Bonus payment	£270	*[2,700 - (630 x 4) units] x £1.50*
= Total cost	£6,970	

Note how the second method from the previous page (basic pay and overtime) is used here to work out the answers.

labour costs – direct or indirect?

The rule that **direct costs** are those that can be identified directly with each unit of output applies to labour costs. Therefore . . .

■ the pay for **production operatives** will generally be classed as **direct costs**

■ the pay for **production supervisors** and **non-production employees** will be treated as **indirect costs**

But . . .

■ **overtime premium** paid to **production operatives** is usually classed as an **indirect cost** because it is not normally linked to specific units but spread over all output along with other overheads

■ an exception to this would be if the overtime was a requirement of a specific urgent job and then the premium would be a legitimate **direct cost** of that job

Also . . .

■ **idle time** is when a worker is paid but is not engaged in production work (eg when machinery breaks down or the employee undergoes training). For production workers **idle time** is also usually treated as an **indirect cost**

7 Dealing with overheads

WHAT IS THE PROBLEM?

The challenge here is to spread the cost of overheads fairly over the output of the organisation. The first three steps are explained in this chapter, with the final step – absorption – explained in the following chapter. The overall process will enable you to work out the amount of indirect costs that relate to each unit produced.

the steps in the process

The diagram below illustrates all four steps involved:

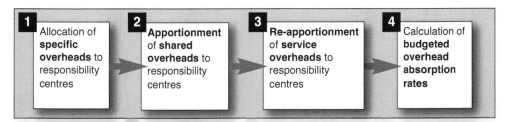

1 Allocation of **specific overheads** to responsibility centres

2 **Apportionment** of **shared overheads** to responsibility centres

3 **Re-apportionment** of **service overheads** to responsibility centres

4 Calculation of **budgeted overhead absorption rates**

the steps explained

These steps are used to analyse budgeted production overhead costs so that a **budgeted overhead absorption rate** can be calculated. This can then be used to provide a value for indirect costs in products and services under absorption costing.

Step 1: allocation of specific costs to responsibility centres

- Some indirect costs clearly relate to only one responsibility centre – for example the salary of a supervisor in the packing department.
- These costs are allocated direct to the relevant centre, eg the packing department.

Step 2: apportionment of shared overheads to responsibility centres

- Indirect costs that relate to more than one responsibility centre must be shared between these centres using a fair method to apportion the costs.
- For example heating costs could use comparative floor areas to work out the proportion of the total cost that should be applied to each responsibility centre.

Note that these first two steps may be carried out at the same time, depending on how the information is presented. Step 3 is explained on the next page.

Step 3: re-apportionment of service overheads to responsibility centres

- The first two steps are likely to result in costs being allocated and apportioned to **service cost centres**. These are responsibility centres that are not involved in the production of finished products but instead provide support to the production responsibility centres.

- Examples of **service cost centres** are stores and cleaning services. In order for these costs to be shared across the finished products, they must be re-apportioned to the responsibility centres that benefit from their services.

- An example of data to use to re-apportion stores costs could be the number of issues to each production responsibility centre. If the fabrication department received twice as many issues as the assembly department it would bear twice as much cost.

Step 4: calculation of budgeted overhead absorption rate

- The previous three steps will have resulted in **all** the indirect production costs being allocated to the responsibility centres that are involved in direct production.

- These cost totals can then be used to calculate absorption rates. This process is explained in the next chapter.

The extended worked examples that follow show how allocation, apportionment and re-apportionment (Steps 1, 2 and 3) are carried out.

EXAMPLE – apportionment of costs – data

A factory has three responsibility centres, with the following data available:

Responsibility Centre	Floor space (Square metres)	Non-current assets (Carrying value £)	Stores Issues to (Number)
Assembly	800	30,000	7,500
Finishing	400	10,000	2,500
Stores	400	20,000	-

The **budgeted overheads** for the period are as follows:

		£
Rent		40,000
Indirect labour:	Assembly	25,000
	Finishing	15,000
	Stores	34,000
Depreciation		12,000
Other property overheads		24,000

EXAMPLE – the decisions to be made

- The first decision is to see which budgeted costs can be allocated and which need to be apportioned:
  - the **indirect labour costs** clearly all relate to specific responsibility centres and can therefore be allocated straightaway
  - **other costs** relate to more than one centre and so must be apportioned

- Now you need to decide which data is most suitable for apportioning each relevant cost. In this simple example there are limited choices:
  - **rent** normally relates to the size of the building; it therefore makes sense to use the floor space to apportion the cost to the responsibility centres
  - **depreciation** relates to the non-current assets; in the absence of more specific information the assets' carrying value is the most appropriate data
  - **other property overheads** relate to the building and so floor space seems the most appropriate data to use

We will now show how these decisions are implemented, before going on to examine the re-apportionment of the stores costs, as it is a service cost centre.

EXAMPLE (steps 1 & 2) – the allocation and apportionment calculations

This table below shows how the decisions on the previous page are put into practice:

Overhead	Basis	Total £	Assembly £	Finishing £	Stores £
Rent	Floor space	40,000	20,000	10,000	10,000
Indirect Labour	Allocation	74,000	25,000	15,000	34,000
Depreciation	Carrying value	12,000	6,000	2,000	4,000
Other Property	Floor space	24,000	12,000	6,000	6,000
Subtotals		150,000	63,000	33,000	54,000

Example: apportionment of rent is calculated as follows:

Total floor space of the factory = 800 + 400 + 400 = 1,600 square metres.

The total rent of £40,000 is apportioned to each responsibility centre using the proportion of this total space that it occupies:

Assembly	£40,000 x (800 ÷ 1,600)	= £20,000
Finishing	£40,000 x (400 ÷ 1,600)	= £10,000
Stores	£40,000 x (400 ÷ 1,600)	= £10,000

Apportionments of the other overhead costs are calculated using the proportions in each responsibility centre of the relevant total (ie carrying value or floor space).

EXAMPLE (step 3) – the re-apportionment of stores costs

You now need to decide how to **re-apportion** the stores costs and carry out the necessary calculations.

- Stores is a service cost centre and not directly involved in production.
- The total cost of stores needs to be re-apportioned, based on the benefit that it provides to the production responsibility centres that it services.
- The best available data to use for this is the number of **stores issues**.

The starting point of the calculation is the subtotals line from the table on the last page:

	Basis	Total £	Assembly £	Finishing £	Stores £
Subtotals (b/f)		150,000	63,000	33,000	54,000
Re-apportionment of stores total cost	number of issues		40,500	13,500	(54,000)*
Totals		150,000*	103,500	46,500	0

The re-apportionment calculation uses the same approach as before, but this time using the share of the total issues. Assembly (for example) is calculated as:

£54,000 x (7,500 ÷ 10,000) = £40,500.

*Note: total Stores cost is deducted, leaving the amount in the Total column unchanged.

re-apportionment of overheads – some more detail

▓ **direct method**

Re-apportionment can be straightforward, as in the last worked example where the cost of a service cost centre is spread directly over the production centres. This is known as the 'direct method'.

▓ **step-down apportionment**

A more complicated situation can arise when there are several service cost centres, and one (or more) of them may benefit **another service cost centre** as well as production cost centres. In this case you must deal with the re-apportionment of any service cost centres that benefit other service cost centres first. This is known as 'step-down' apportionment.

EXAMPLE – step-down apportionment

There are two service cost centres:
Maintenance benefits only the production centres.
Canteen benefits the maintenance cost centre as well as the production centres.

The order of re-apportionment is:

1 **Canteen** – this will add to **maintenance** and also the other responsibility centres
2 **Maintenance** – the increased total cost is re-apportioned to the production centres

---

8 Absorption of overheads

CHARGING THE COSTS TO THE PRODUCTS

In the last chapter we showed how budgeted indirect costs are charged to production responsibility centres. This involved steps 1 to 3 shown in the diagram on page 32.

Now we explain the final stage, step 4, in which these costs are used to calculate overhead absorption rates which can be applied to the products.

the budgeted overhead absorption rate

- The **absorption rate** is a mechanism for charging some of the total budgeted costs in each production centre to products that are made there.

- The total budgeted costs for a production centre are divided by selected budgeted data (for example the number of labour hours worked in that centre) to calculate the **budgeted overhead absorption rate**.

  For example, if labour hours had been used the absorption rate would be expressed in '£ per labour hour'.

main absorption bases

Each budgeted overhead absorption rate uses an **absorption base** that is decided on by examining the relevant production centre and the way in which it operates.

▨ direct labour hours

This 'base' can be used for production which is labour-intensive. The absorption rate is calculated by dividing the budgeted overheads by the budgeted number of direct labour hours.

Budgeted absorption rate per direct labour hour =

$$\frac{budgeted\ overheads\ for\ production\ centre}{budgeted\ direct\ labour\ hours\ for\ production\ centre}$$

▨ direct labour percentage

A percentage is calculated that can be added to the direct labour cost to represent the overheads. It is useful when labour rates differ considerably.

Budgeted absorption rate as direct labour percentage =

$$\frac{budgeted\ overheads\ for\ production\ centre}{budgeted\ direct\ labour\ cost\ for\ production\ centre} \times 100$$

▓ machine hours

This base is useful for machine-intensive operations and where a large part of the overheads relates to the cost of operating machinery.

It is calculated by dividing budgeted overheads by budgeted machine hours.

Budgeted absorption rate per machine hour =

budgeted overheads for the production centre

budgeted machine hours for the production centre

▓ volume bases

These are often used by service sector organisations. An example is miles travelled by a bus company.

This base is calculated by dividing the budgeted overheads by the budgeted chosen volume, for example budgeted miles for a bus company:

Budgeted absorption rate per mile travelled =

budgeted overheads for the bus company

budgeted miles travelled by the bus company

EXAMPLE (step 4) – using absorption rates

This example uses the budgeted costs from the previous worked example (see pages 35-38) and additional information to illustrate the calculation of the most appropriate hourly absorption rates to apply to the two production centres, Assembly and Finishing:

Centre	Total	Budgeted Direct Labour Hours	Budgeted Machine Hours
Assembly	£103,500	3,000	15,000
Finishing	£ 46,500	9,300	0

Assembly is machine-intensive because it has many more budgeted machine hours than budgeted direct labour hours. Therefore **machine hours** is likely to be the most appropriate absorption base. This is calculated as:

£103,500 ÷ 15,000 hours = £6.90 per machine hour

Finishing involves only labour, so the appropriate absorption base is **labour hours**. This is calculated as:

£46,500 ÷ 9,300 hours = £5.00 per direct labour hour

absorption of overheads

When the budgeted information has been used to calculate the budgeted overhead absorption rates, these rates are used to charge (absorb) overheads to products or services.

Because the rates are based on budgeted figures that may not be entirely accurate, discrepancies – under-absorption or over-absorption – may arise by the end of the period.

■ Under-absorption

Under-absorption arises when the actual overheads for the period are greater than the total absorbed into all the products or services. If this occurs the difference must be debited to the statement of profit or loss as an extra cost. This means that product costs during the period were actually greater than expected.

■ Over-absorption

Over-absorption is the opposite – more overheads have been absorbed into products than the overheads actually cost. This will result in a credit to the statement of profit or loss, as costs have been overstated during the period.

There will always be a small amount of over-absorption or under-absorption, but large amounts mean that the costing data (and maybe the costing system) should be reviewed.

EXAMPLE – absorption of overheads

This example uses the data from the previous example to demonstrate how overheads are absorbed by products, and how under-absorption or over-absorption of overheads can occur. The data is as follows:

Budgeted overheads:	Assembly	£103,500
	Finishing	£46,500
Budgeted machine hours:	Assembly	15,000
Budgeted direct labour hours:	Finishing	9,300
Budgeted overhead absorption rate:	Assembly	£6.90 per machine hour
Budgeted overhead absorption rate:	Finishing	£5.00 per direct labour hour

The company makes two products, Product A and Product B:

Product A needs 2 machine hours in Assembly and 1 direct labour hour in Finishing

Product B needs 5 machine hours in Assembly and 4 direct labour hours in Finishing

EXAMPLE (continued) – calculation of overhead cost in each product

During the period the company made 3,000 units of Product A and 1,800 units of Product B.

Product A

In each unit of Product A, there will be absorbed:

Assembly overheads: £6.90 x 2 machine hours	=	£13.80
Finishing overheads: £5.00 x 1 direct labour hour	=	£ 5.00
Total overheads absorbed into each unit of Product A		£18.80

Product B

In each unit of Product B, there will be absorbed:

Assembly overheads: £6.90 x 5 machine hours	=	£34.50
Finishing overheads: £5.00 x 4 direct labour hours	=	£20.00
Total overheads absorbed into each unit of Product B		£54.50

actual overhead costs incurred

You are now told that during the period the actual overheads incurred were:

Assembly £100,000 and Finishing £53,000.

calculation of over-absorption and under-absorption

The calculation of the overheads of each responsibility centre that are absorbed into the products made are as follows:

		Assembly	Finishing
		£	£
Product A:			
Assembly:	3,000 x £13.80	41,400	
Finishing:	3,000 x £5.00		15,000
Product B:			
Assembly	1,800 x £34.50	62,100	
Finishing	1,800 x £20.00		36,000
Total overheads absorbed:		103,500	51,000
Comparison with the actual cost of overheads:		100,000	53,000
Assembly is **over-absorbed**:		3,500	
Finishing is **under-absorbed**:			2,000

Conclusion: under-absorption in Finishing means that not all the actual overheads have been accounted for – the £2,000 must be ultimately debited to the statement of profit or loss. Over-absorption in Assembly means that more costs were absorbed than were actually incurred, so £3,500 will be credited to the statement of profit or loss.

9 Cost bookkeeping

DEBITS AND CREDITS FOR COSTING

Cost bookkeeping follows the same general rules as other areas of double-entry bookkeeping.

You need to make sure that you can apply these rules to account for costing transactions.

areas which involve cost bookkeeping

The main areas that you need to deal with are those already explained in this Guide:

- **accounting for materials** – purchase of inventory and issues from stores to production

- **accounting for labour** – linking the payroll accounting system with the analysis of labour costs

- **accounting for overheads** – absorption of overheads and the treatment of under-absorption and over-absorption

accounting for materials

Materials are purchased and entered into the Inventory account; then as they are issued from stores they are transferred to a Production account (usually as a direct cost).

The **journal entries** will be:

Purchase of inventory: **Debit** specific Inventory account
                                          Credit Bank or Purchase ledger control account

Transfer to production: **Debit** relevant Production account
                                          Credit specific Inventory account

Note that a variety of names for accounts and/or relevant coding may be used.

EXAMPLE – accounting for materials

A manufacturing company uses the following codes for some of its accounts:

Description	Code
Raw materials – Rubber compound	1200
Raw materials – Plastic pellets	1300
Raw materials – 5mm steel cable	1400
Bank	3000
Purchases ledger control	5000
Wages control	6000
Production direct material costs	7100
Production direct labour costs	7200
Production indirect material costs	7300
Production indirect labour costs	7400
Non-production indirect material costs	8300
Non-production indirect labour costs	8400

EXAMPLE – accounting for materials (continued)

The following two transactions took place. The journals that are used to record each transaction are shown below. VAT is ignored.

▨ The purchase (on credit) into inventory of 5,000 kilos of plastic pellets at a cost of £5.80 per kilo.

	Code	Debit (£)	Credit (£)
Raw materials – Plastic pellets	1300	29,000	
Purchasse ledger control	5000		29,000

▨ The transfer from inventory into production of 2,500 kilos of rubber compound, valued at £4.00 per kilo. Rubber compound is used directly in production.

	Code	Debit (£)	Credit (£)
Production direct material costs	7100	10,000	
Raw materials – Rubber compound	1200		10,000

accounting for labour

Payroll is normally analysed through a Wages control account.

The cost of direct and indirect labour can then be transferred to the relevant Production account (direct or indirect) or Non-production account (indirect).

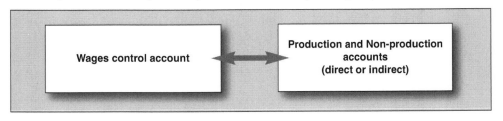

The **journal entries** will be:

    Debit   **Direct production account** (with relevant part of labour cost)

    Debit   **Production overhead account** (with relevant part of labour cost)

    Debit   **Non-production overhead account** (with relevant part of labour cost)

    Credit   **Wages control account** (with total labour costs)

EXAMPLE – accounting for labour

A manufacturing company uses the following codes for its labour cost accounts:

Description	Code
Wages control	6000
Production direct labour costs	7200
Production indirect labour costs	7400
Non-production indirect labour costs	8400

The total **cost of salaries and wages for the month** was £83,860, made up of the following:

Salaries of office managers and staff	£38,560
Wages of production supervisors	£11,200
Wages of production operatives	£34,100

The individual **journal entries** to record these transactions are shown on the next page.

Salaries of office managers and staff

	Code	Debit (£)	Credit (£)
Non-production indirect labour costs	8400	38,560	
Wages control	6000		38,560

Wages of production supervisors

	Code	Debit (£)	Credit (£)
Production indirect labour costs	7400	11,200	
Wages control	6000		11,200

Wages of production operatives

	Code	Debit (£)	Credit (£)
Production direct labour costs	7200	34,100	
Wages control	6000		34,100

accounting for overheads

The actual overhead costs are debited to the relevant Overheads account (or Overheads control account) as they are incurred. The absorbed overheads are credited to this account and debited to a Production account. The final balance on the Overheads account will represent the over-absorption or under-absorption of overheads.

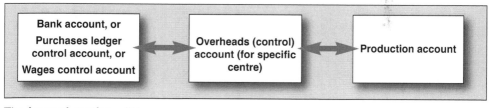

The **journal entries** will be:

Build up of actual costs:	**Debit** relevant Overheads account
	Credit Bank / Purchase ledger control / Wages control
Absorption of overheads:	**Debit** relevant Production account
	Credit relevant Overheads account
Over- (under-) absorption:	**Debit** (or Credit) relevant Overheads account
	Credit (or Debit) statement of profit or loss

EXAMPLE – accounting for overheads

A manufacturing company makes two products – Ayeprod and Beeprod.
The company uses the following codes for some of its cost accounts:

Description	Code
Total cost of Ayeprod production	9000
Total cost of Beeprod production	9200
Production overheads control account	9500
Statement of profit or loss	9900

The month-end balance of the Production overheads control account is £231,560 debit. This represents the actual total production overheads incurred during the month.

During the month:

- 3,600 units of Ayeprod were produced
- Each unit of Ayeprod absorbs £28 of production overhead
- 5,400 units of Beeprod were produced
- Each unit of Beeprod absorbs £23 of production overhead

The absorption of overheads has not yet been recorded in the cost accounts.

The journal entries to record the absorption of overheads will be as follows:

	Code	Debit (£)	Credit (£)
Total cost of Ayeprod production	9000	100,800	
Production overheads control account	9500		100,800
Total cost of Beeprod production	9200	124,200	
Production overheads control account	9500		124,200

These transactions will result in a debit balance on the Production overheads control account of £6,560 (ie £231,560 – £100,800 – £124,200).

This represents under-absorption of overheads for the month, because the amounts absorbed are less than the overheads actually incurred. This balance will be transferred (as an additional cost) to the statement of profit or loss as follows:

	Code	Debit (£)	Credit (£)
Statement of profit or loss	9900	6,560	
Production overheads control account	9500		6,560

10 Specific costing methods

WHY THE DIFFERENT METHODS?

Costing systems are put in place to help managers to run their organisations.

There are many different methods of costing.

The activities that organisations carry out vary, and so an organisation should choose the method of costing that best meets its needs.

methods of costing

The main types of costing are listed below and explained in full on the next three pages.

- **unit costing** – used where a large number of units of each product are produced
- **job costing** – used where each 'job' undertaken by a business is different
- **batch costing** – used where batches of products are made to different specifications
- **service costing** – used where the organisation provides a service
- **process costing** – used where production is continuous

- **unit costing**

    - calculates the cost of each individual unit

    - is the costing method that has been illustrated so far in this book

    - is most suited for organisations that produce several different products and in large quantities

      Examples: a furniture manufacturer, a car component manufacturer

- **job costing**

    - is used where each product or service that is produced is a 'one-off' job

    - collects together all the costs for that particular job

    - each job will normally have a different cost based on the customer's individual requirements

      Examples: a fitted kitchen, a car repair, a wedding reception

▨ batch costing

- a variation of unit costing that is used when items are made in batches

- the items in the batch are identical, and the costs calculated for the whole batch

- a batch of a particular product will often be made and then discontinued in order to make way for production of another and different batch

  Examples: 'new season' fashion clothing, a 'special edition' car, a type of pizza

▨ service costing

- a costing method that is used in service industries

- useful where there are continuous activities that can be thought of as multiples of a simple measure of output

  Example: 'cost per passenger mile' for a bus company

■ **process costing**

- used where manufacture involves a continuous process which may never (or rarely) stop

- this costing method is dealt with in much more detail in the next chapter

Example: the manufacture of chocolate bars

11 Process costing

WHAT IS SO DIFFERENT ABOUT PROCESS COSTING?

In its simplest form process costing involves collecting all the costs and dividing the total by the total output for the period to get a cost per unit.

But, as we will see in this chapter, process costing becomes more difficult when work-in-progress and normal and abnormal losses are involved in the calculations.

process costing – the basics

Process costing is used for **continuous processes,** which means the costs are worked out for a **period of time**.

The total costs for the period are then divided by the total output for the same period to give a cost per unit of output (cost unit):

$$cost\ per\ cost\ unit\ =\ \frac{total\ costs\ of\ the\ process\ for\ the\ period}{total\ cost\ units\ for\ the\ period}$$

The example which follows shows, step-by-step, how process costing works.

EXAMPLE – process costing

The 'FudgeChoc' confectionary bar is produced using two processes which operate continuously. The first process involves making the fudge centre of the product, and the second produces the chocolate which is used to coat the fudge.

During the month of November 7,300,000 FudgeChoc bars were produced with process costs as follows:

Process 1 (Fudge)	£	Process 2 (Choc)	£
Materials	500,000	Materials	340,000
Direct labour	124,000	Direct labour	180,000
Production overheads	186,000	Production overheads	130,000
	810,000		650,000

Total costs of the two processes: £810,000 + £650,000 = £1,460,000

Cost per bar of FudgeChoc: $\dfrac{£1,460,000}{7,300,000}$ = £0.20 per bar

dealing with work-in-progress

In the FudgeChoc example on the previous page it is assumed that the product is started and finished in the given period.

But this is not always the case and you will have to deal with part-completed items, ie the **work-in-progress** at the end of the given period.

So that you can share out the costs of the process in a fair way you will need to know the **degree of completeness** of these unfinished products so that you can calculate the number of **equivalent units** for costing purposes. The formula for this is:

number of part-completed units x percentage of completeness = number of equivalent units

> Example: 200 units which are 50% complete, the calculation is:
>
> 200 units x 50% = <u>100 equivalent units</u>

a further complication – adjusting for materials, labour and overheads

The example above assumes that all the elements of cost – materials, labour and overheads – are all at the same level of completeness, but in reality these three percentages of completion may be different. For example, the materials completion percentage may be 90%, the labour percentage 40% and the overheads percentage 40%.

The method of dealing with this situation is illustrated in the worked example which follows.

EXAMPLE – process costing involving work-in-progress

At the start of January, Supajuice Ltd, a company that produces fruit juice for supermarkets, had no work-in-progress following the Christmas break.

At the end of January 564,000 litres had been processed, and an additional 40,000 litres were still in process as follows:

> 90% materials used
>
> 40% direct labour used
>
> 40% overheads used

During January the process incurred the following costs:

Direct materials	£21,000
Direct labour	£46,400
Overheads	£40,600
Total	£108,000

You are to calculate the cost per equivalent unit (litre), and also the total cost of the completed January production and of the work-in-progress (see next page).

Cost per equivalent unit (litre)

This can be worked out using the formula:

total cost ÷ (completed units + equivalent units in progress) = cost per equivalent unit

	total cost		equivalent units	workings of cost per equivalent unit		cost per unit (£)
Direct materials	£21,000	÷	600,000	564,000 + (90% x 40,000)	=	0.035
Direct labour	£46,400	÷	580,000	564,000 + (40% x 40,000)	=	0.080
Overheads	£40,600	÷	580,000	564,000 + (40% x 40,000)	=	0.070
						0.185

Cost of completed production:

£0.185 x 564,000 units = £104,340

Cost of work-in-progress:

Direct materials	£0.035 x (40,000 x 90%)	=	£1,260
Direct labour	£0.080 x (40,000 x 40%)	=	£1,280
Overheads	£0.070 x (40,000 x 40%)	=	£1,120
			£3,660

Note that the cost of completed production of £104,340, plus the cost of closing work-in-progress of £3,660 equals the total costs of the period of £108,000.

The closing work-in-progress will form the opening work-in-progress for the next period.

the Process account

The **Process account** is used to record process costing and is the equivalent of the Production account.

The costs of the inputs to the process are debited to the Process account, and the account is subsequently credited when the total costs of the finished goods are transferred to the Finished goods account.

The figures from the worked example on the previous page are used below to illustrate a simple Process account.

Dr		**Process Account**		Cr
	£			£
Direct materials	21,000			
Direct labour	46,400	Finished goods	104,340	
Overheads	40,600	Work-in-progress c/d	3,660	
	108,000		108,000	

Process accounts often also contain additional columns with details of quantities and units costs as we will see later in this chapter.

process losses and gains

Processes often result in losses through wastage of material, and this has to be taken into account. The cost of the 'good' output is calculated by deducting the amount of the normal loss caused by wastage and adding back any scrap value income.

Scrap value is the amount of money that can be realised if waste products from the process are sold.

> *Example:*
> *A business that makes oven chips will account for a certain weight of potatoes, but will expect to lose some of that weight when the potatoes are peeled. The peelings may then be sold at **scrap value**.*

The loss in a process can be classified as a **normal loss** or an **abnormal loss**.

- **Normal losses** are those **expected** (planned for) from the process.

  The cost of the losses can be offset by income – the **scrap value** – that may be received from the sale of the wastage. This scrap value will be accounted for in the Process account.

  > *Example:*
  > *The oven chips normal (expected) loss is 10%, so for every 100kg of potatoes input, 10kg will be lost but this may then be offset by the sale of the peelings.*

■ **Abnormal losses** are losses **in excess of any normal losses**. As they are unexpected they are accounted for separately by valuing the abnormal loss at the same unit cost as the expected good output. This abnormal loss will be offset by any scrap value of just the abnormal part of the loss.

Example:
If the oven chips' normal (expected) loss from peeling is 10% for every 100kg of potatoes, but the actual loss is 15%, the abnormal loss will be:

15% actual loss minus 10% normal loss = 5% abnormal (unexpected loss).

■ **Abnormal gains** occur when the output from the process is greater than would be expected. This is because the actual loss is less than the normal (expected) loss. The difference between the normal loss and the actual loss is accounted for as an abnormal gain in a similar (but opposite) way to abnormal losses.

Example:
If 100kg of potatoes in the process produce 8 kg of peel rather than the normal 10kg, the abnormal gain will be 10kg minus 8kg, ie 2kg of peel.

We will now illustrate normal and abnormal losses and abnormal gains and their accounting treatment in two extended worked examples.

EXAMPLE – normal and abnormal losses

A process involves inputting 20,000 kg of material. There are normal losses of 2,000 kg, so the expected good output is 18,000 kg.

The costs incurred in the process during a period are:

Direct materials	£60,000
Direct labour	£25,000
Overheads	£25,000
Total costs	£110,000

The actual output during the period was 17,500 kg due to abnormal losses of 500 kg.

All the losses (normal and abnormal) are sold for scrap at £1 per kg.

The cost per unit of the expected output is calculated as follows:

(Input costs – scrap value of normal loss) ÷ expected output

(£110,000 – (2,000kg x £1)) ÷ 18,000kg = £6.00 per kg

This is used to value the actual output: 17,500kg x £6.00 = £105,000.

The abnormal loss is initially valued at the same cost per unit as the expected output: 500kg x £6.00 = £3,000.

This is then reduced to £2,500 by deducting the scrap income of £500.

The Process account then appears as follows:

Process Account							
Details	Qty kg	Unit cost £	Total cost £	Details	Qty kg	Unit cost £	Total cost £
Direct materials	20,000	3.00	60,000	Normal loss	2,000	1.00	2,000
Direct labour		1.25	25,000	Finished goods	17,500	6.00	105,000
Overheads		1.25	25,000	Abnormal loss	500	6.00	3,000
	20,000		110,000		20,000		110,000

Note carefully how the figures on the Process accounts are arrived at:

▪ The normal loss credit entry of £2,000 results from the normal scrap income.

▪ The Abnormal loss account will be:
  – debited with the £3,000 from the Process account, and
  – credited with income of £500 from the additional scrap income

The net debit balance of £2,500 on the Abnormal loss account will be transferred as a debit to the statement of profit or loss.

EXAMPLE – normal losses and abnormal gains

We will now use a modified example to show how abnormal gains are dealt with.

A process involves the use of 20,000kg of material.

There are normal losses of 2,000kg, so the expected output is 18,000kg.

The costs incurred in the process during a period are:

Direct materials	£60,000
Direct labour	£25,000
Overheads	£25,000
Total costs	£110,000

The actual output during the period was 18,200kg due to abnormal gains of 200kg.

All losses are sold for scrap at £1 per kg.

The cost per unit of the expected output is calculated as previously:

(Input costs – scrap value of normal loss) ÷ expected output

(£110,000 – £2,000) ÷ 18,000 kg = £6.00 per kg

This is used to value the actual output: 18,200kg x £6.00 = £109,200

The abnormal gain is shown in the Process account at 200kg x £6.00 = £1,200.

The Process account then appears as follows:

Process Account							
Details	Qty kg	Unit cost £	Total cost £	Details	Qty kg	Unit cost £	Total cost £
Direct materials	20,000	3.00	60,000	Normal loss	2,000	1.00	2,000
Direct labour		1.25	25,000	Finished goods	18,200	6.00	109,200
Overheads		1.25	25,000				
Abnormal gain	200	6.00	1,200				
	20,200		111,200		20,200		111,200

Note how the figures are arrived at:

The Abnormal gain account will be

- debited with £200 from the Normal loss account due to the reduced scrap value receivable, and
- credited with the £1,200 from the Process account

The net credit balance of £1,000 on the Abnormal gain account (equalling 200kg x (£6.00 – £1.00 reduced scrap)) will be transferred as a credit in the statement of profit or loss.

12 Cost behaviour

HOW DO COSTS BEHAVE?

The topic of cost behaviour examines how costs can change in the short term when the level of output changes.

Remember! These cost categories relate to what happens to the total costs – not the costs per unit.

the categories of cost

There are four main categories of cost:

- **fixed costs** – which remain the same when output changes

- **variable costs** – which vary in line with the level of output

- **stepped fixed costs** – costs which increase in 'steps' as output increases

- **semi-variable costs** – costs which include both fixed costs and also variable costs

These four categories are explained and illustrated with graphs on the next two pages.

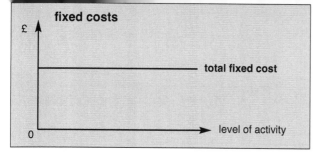

A cost is described as a **fixed cost** if the total cost does not change when the level of activity changes.

Example: factory rent

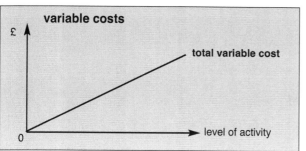

A cost is described as a **variable cost** if the total cost varies in direct proportion to the level of activity.

Example: direct material

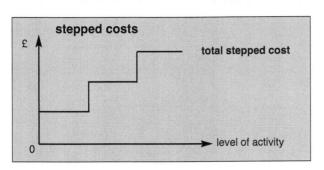

A cost is described as a **stepped cost** if its total changes in steps at certain levels of activity, but remains unchanged in between.

Example: the cost of taking on an extra supervisor when production increases.

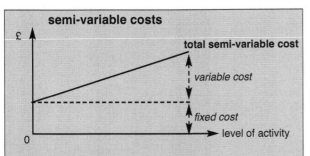

A cost is described as a **semi-variable cost** if the total cost is made up of a variable part and a fixed part.

Example: a telephone bill which includes a line rental (fixed) and a unit cost for each call (variable).

analysing semi-variable costs

If we have information about the total semi-variable costs at two different activity levels we can analyse the costs into the fixed and variable elements using the 'high-low' method. The two activity levels chosen are normally a 'high' one and a 'low' one. This method then allows us to use these figures to predict total costs at other activity levels.

calculation method

1 Calculate the differences between two sets (high and low) of
   - cost totals, and
   - activity levels

2 Divide the cost difference by the activity difference to obtain the **variable cost per unit** of activity.
   Then choose one of the cost totals and use the variable cost per unit to calculate the amount of **variable costs contained within the total costs.**

3 Deduct these **variable costs** from the total cost . . . the result will be the **fixed cost.**

   We now have the fixed cost (in total) and the variable cost (per unit) and these can be used to calculate the total costs at other activity levels. This type of calculation is shown in a worked example on the next page.

EXAMPLE – analysing semi-variable costs

1 You are given the total costs for two different levels of output of units.
   You then calculate the differences between the two sets of figures:

	Units	Total costs (£)
	9,900	162,250
minus	6,400	136,000
Differences:	3,500	26,250

You will see from this that it costs £26,250 to produce an additional 3,500 units.

This is all **variable cost**.

2 Using the difference figures you can then calculate the **variable cost per unit**:

£26,250 ÷ 3,500 = £7.50 per unit

Using this figure of £7.50 per unit you can now work out the variable costs
contained in the total cost of producing one of these two output levels.

In this case if you take the higher total, ie 9,900 units, the variable costs will be:

9,900 (units) x £7.50 (variable cost per unit) = £74,250

3 The next step is to work out the **fixed cost** element. We will use the output level of 9,900 units and the formula: *total costs – variable costs = fixed costs*

	£
Total cost of 9,900 units (see step 1 above)	162,250
minus variable costs (9,900 units x £7.50)	74,250
= **fixed cost:**	88,000

This process then can be used to calculate total costs for other levels of output.

sample further calculation based on the example figures shown above:

We know the variable costs are £7.50 per unit and the fixed costs are £88,000.

The total cost at (say) 8,000 units will therefore be:

	£
Variable costs (£7.50 x 8,000)	60,000
Fixed costs	88,000
Total costs	148,000

13 Marginal and absorption costing

WHAT IS THE DIFFERENCE?

Marginal costing and absorption costing are two different methods of costing, and are used for two different purposes.

Marginal costing is largely based on variable costs rather than on fixed costs and works out the cost of producing one extra unit of output; it is useful for decision making by management.

*Absorption costing incorporates variable costs **and fixed costs** into the cost of producing one unit of output (as explained in Chapter 7).*

key features – marginal costing

- ▨ separates variable costs from fixed costs
- ▨ values products or services only using variable costs
- ▨ treats fixed costs (eg annual rent) as relating to periods of time, not products
- ▨ calculates 'contribution' as selling price less variable costs
- ▨ is especially useful for short-term decision making

key features – absorption costing

- analyses costs by element and nature (direct/indirect)
- absorbs indirect costs into products or services
- uses pre-determined rates and so can be imprecise
- provides a product cost that includes **all** costs of production
- is used in financial statements for inventory valuation

cost analysis and terminology – marginal and absorption costing

The types of cost data used by the two costing methods are shown in this diagram:

marginal costing	absorption costing
variable costs variable direct materials, labour, expenses and overheads	**direct costs** direct materials, labour expenses
fixed costs fixed direct expenses fixed overheads	**indirect costs** variable overheads fixed overheads

profit statements – using marginal and absorption costing

There are differences in approach and terminology between marginal and absorption costing and so the profit statements using each method of costing also differ.

The worked example set out below highlights these differences.

EXAMPLE – profit statement comparison

■ A business manufactures desks with costs as follows:

Direct materials	£18 per desk
Direct labour	£12 per desk
Fixed production overheads	£15 per desk

■ Direct costs are all variable.

■ The overheads are based on making 1,000 desks in a period with fixed production overheads of £15,000 in that period.

■ During the period the business made 1,000 desks and sold them all for £70 each.

■ There was no opening or closing inventory.

The profit statements using marginal and absorption costing appear as shown below.

MARGINAL COSTING Profit Statement	£	ABSORPTION COSTING Profit Statement	£
Sales revenue	70,000	Sales revenue	70,000
Less variable costs:		Direct costs:	
Materials	18,000	Materials	18,000
Labour	12,000	Labour	12,000
	30,000		30,000
Contribution	40,000	Indirect costs of production	15,000
Less fixed costs:	15,000	Total production costs	45,000
Profit	25,000	Profit	25,000

in this example . . .

■ the two statements use different layouts and terminology

■ the resulting profits are identical

■ the profits would be different using the two methods of costing if there are changes in inventory levels over the period

inventories and reported profits

The valuation of inventories using marginal costing differs from the valuation of inventory using absorption costing:

- **marginal costing** – inventory is valued at **variable cost**

- **absorption costing** – inventory is valued at **absorbed cost**

This means that when there are changes in the levels of inventory during the period (between opening and closing inventory) there will be a difference in the reported profit using each of the two costing methods.

> **EXAMPLE – marginal and absorption costing: differences in profit levels**
>
> Using data from the example on the previous page, any closing inventory would be valued as follows:
>
> - under **marginal costing**: £18 + £12 = £30 per desk
>
> - under **absorption costing**: £18 + £12 + £15* = £45 per desk
>   *overheads of (£15,000 ÷ 1,000 desks) = £15
>
> Suppose that in the period 1,000 desks were made, but only 800 were sold, leaving a closing inventory of 200 desks.
>
> The profit statements would then appear as shown below.

MARGINAL COSTING Profit Statement		ABSORPTION COSTING Profit Statement	
	£		£
Sales revenue (800 x £70)	56,000	Sales revenue (800 x £70)	56,000
Less variable costs:		Direct costs:	
Materials	18,000	Materials	18,000
Labour	12,000	Labour	12,000
	30,000		30,000
Less closing inventory (200 x £30):	6,000	Indirect costs of production	15,000
Variable cost of sales	24,000	Total production costs	45,000
		Less closing inventory (200 x £45)	9,000
Contribution	32,000	Production cost of sales	36,000
Less fixed costs:	15,000		
Profit	17,000	Profit	20,000

Note: in this second example the absorption costing approach has included (£15 x 200) = £3,000 of fixed costs in inventory and carried these costs into the next period. This amount accounts for the difference in profit between the two methods.

14 Activity based costing

A THIRD METHOD OF COSTING

There are some situations where neither marginal costing nor absorption costing will provide the most useful information. Activity based costing (ABC) is a development of absorption costing that charges overheads to production on the basis of activities.

key features – activity based costing

- provides a more accurate way of charging overheads to cost units
- identifies the activities that cause overheads to be incurred
- identifies appropriate 'cost drivers' for each of these activities
- charges overheads to cost units based on how activities are used
- copes well when costing products that are made in different ways (for example in different batch sizes)

Activity	Cost driver
Set-up of production equipment	Number of set-ups
Issuing components to production	Number of issues
Quality control inspections	Number of inspections

If we know how much it costs to carry out an activity, and what the cost driver is, we can calculate how much of this overhead to charge to each cost unit.

For example if it costs £120,000 per year to set up production equipment, and there are 48 set-ups carried out (the cost driver) then each production set up cost is £120,000 / 48 = £2,500.

A product made in small batches of 10 items that requires one set-up per batch will incur a set-up cost of £2,500 / 10 = £250 per unit.

A product made in large batches of 1,000 items that requires one set-up per batch will incur a set-up cost of £2,500 / 1,000 = £2.50 per unit.

15 Budgeting

USING BUDGETS

Budgets are financial plans prepared by organisations; they can be fixed or flexible.

Budgets are prepared in advance and are used to compare actual results against budgeted projections.

Any differences (variances) can then be calculated and analysed and appropriate action taken.

the purpose of budgets

- **decision making** – draft budgets can be prepared based on various possible situations so that the best options can be chosen

- **planning** – budgets enable organisations to plan the resources (eg materials) that will be needed in future periods and identify what outcomes can be expected

- **control** – organisations can compare budgeted and actual results and then take the necessary action where there are differences (variances)

fixed and flexible budgets

Fixed budgets and flexible budgets are two key types of budget you need to know about:

- **Fixed budgets** are set for the expected level of activity and remain 'fixed' even if the level of activity changes. They are normally used when the budgeted costs are fixed and not dependent on the activity level.
  Example: an advertising budget can be set in advance and will not be influenced by production levels.

- **Flexible (or flexed) budgets** are prepared when the expected income and/or costs will change when activity levels change.
  Example: the income and costs for operating a restaurant will be very different when the restaurant is nearly empty compared to when it is full of customers.

You need to be able to prepare flexible budgets from an original budget using information about cost behaviour. It is important to remember that you only flex the budget because of different levels of activity – nothing else. Bear in mind that

- **variable costs** vary in proportion to activity (output)
- **fixed costs** are unchanged (within normal output range)

When a flexible budget has been prepared it can be compared with the actual results for the same output level, and any variances calculated and investigated.

creating a flexible budget and calculating variances

If you are asked to create a flexible budget and calculate variances it will normally be because the actual output differs from the budgeted output.

You should create a flexible budget based on the actual activity level by

■ recalculating the budgeted income (if any) for the actual activity level

■ recalculating each budgeted variable cost for the actual activity level

■ leaving unchanged the fixed costs from the original budget

When you have prepared a flexible budget you can then calculate any variances by comparing the flexible budget with the actual figures, remembering that

■ if actual **income** is **higher** than budgeted income the variance is **favourable**

■ if actual **income** is **lower** than budgeted income the variance is **adverse**

■ if actual **costs** are **higher** than the budgeted costs the variances are **adverse**

■ if actual **costs** are **lower** than the budgeted costs the variances are **favourable**

Note that when a **flexible budget** is adjusted it is also known as a **flexed budget**.

EXAMPLE step 1 – preparing a flexed budget – data needed

In this example the original budget was based on making and selling 20,000 units.
All budgeted costs except fixed overheads are variable costs.

When the actual figures became available only 18,000 units had been made and sold.

Therefore a flexed budget based on output of 18,000 units is required. The figures
which will form the basis of the flexed budget are as follows:

	Original Budget 20,000 units £	**Actual figures** 18,000 units £
Revenue	300,000	265,000
Less costs:		
Materials	55,000	51,750
Labour	76,000	66,000
Variable Overheads	79,000	71,500
Fixed Overheads	63,000	61,950
Profit	27,000	13,800

EXAMPLE step 2 – flexing the budget – the calculations

The next step is to flex the budget to the actual output level. The calculation is:

budgeted figure from the original budget x *actual number of units produced*
number of units from original budget

Note that you must only flex the income and costs that change because the level of output has changed. The fixed overhead figure of £63,000 is not flexed.

	Original Budget 20,000 units	Flexed budget 18,000 units	Actual figures 18,000 units
	£	£	£
Revenue	300,000	270,000	265,000
Less costs:			
Materials	55,000	49,500	51,750
Labour	76,000	68,400	66,000
Variable Overheads	79,000	71,100	71,500
Fixed Overheads	63,000	63,000	61,950
Profit	27,000	18,000	13,800

EXAMPLE step 3 – calculating the variances

You now have flexed budget figures and actual figures at the same level of activity: 18,000 units.

You can now calculate the variances between the actual results and the flexed budget figures.

	Flexed budget 18,000 units	Actual 18,000 units	Variance	
	£	£	£	
Revenue	270,000	265,000	5,000	Adv
Less costs:				
Materials	49,500	51,750	2,250	Adv
Labour	68,400	66,000	2,400	Fav
Variable Overheads	71,100	71,500	400	Adv
Fixed Overheads	63,000	61,950	1,050	Fav
Profit	18,000	13,800	4,200	Adv

Note: remember to state whether the variance is adverse or favourable.

16 Break-even analysis

THE PURPOSE OF BREAK-EVEN ANALYSIS

Break-even analysis is a quick method of working out the number of units and the sales income needed to 'break-even' – ie to make zero profit. Any sales above this point will then make some profit.

Break-even analysis can also be used to work out how to achieve a required level of profit or how far planned sales can fall before the business makes a loss.

calculating break-even

The break-even point can be calculated in:

- **the number of units**: = *fixed costs (£) ÷ contribution per unit (£)*
- **sales value (revenue)**: = *fixed costs (£) ÷ contribution per £ of sales*

Remember that 'contribution' is the sales revenue less the variable costs.

The **contribution sales ratio** (C/S ratio) is *contribution per unit (£) ÷ selling price (£)*.

reaching a target profit

The units or revenue (sales value) needed to reach a target profit can be calculated by adding the target profit to the fixed costs before dividing:

- **in number of units**: = *(fixed costs + target profit) ÷ contribution per unit*
- **in revenue**: = *(fixed costs + target profit) ÷ contribution per £ of sales*

margin of safety

When the break-even point is known, the **margin of safety** – the difference between expected output and break-even output – can be calculated in units or in revenue:

- **margin of safety (units)**: = *budgeted sales units – break-even units*
- **margin of safety (revenue)** = *budgeted sales revenue – break-even revenue*

margin of safety percentage

The margin of safety (units or revenue) can also be expressed as a **percentage**. This shows how far output can fall as a percentage of budgeted unit sales before losses are incurred. The formula is:

(margin of safety (units or revenue) ÷ budgeted units or revenue) x 100

Units or revenue must be used consistently, but will both produce the same percentage.

EXAMPLE – break-even analysis

A company has the following unit data for one of its products.
This data is based on budgeted sales of 20,000 units:

	£
Selling price	50
Variable costs:	
Direct materials	12
Direct labour	13
Overheads	10
Fixed costs	12

The **break-even point calculations** are as follows:

The contribution per unit:	£50 – (£12 + £13 + £10) = £15
The fixed costs for the period:	£12 x 20,000 = £240,000
The contribution to sales (C/S) ratio:	£15 ÷ £50 = 0.3

Break-even point (in **units**):	£240,000 ÷ £15	= 16,000 units
Break-even point (in **sales revenue**):	£240,000 ÷ 0.3	= £800,000

checking the figures

As the calculation of the break-even point is in both units and revenue it is possible to check that the figures are consistent, ie 16,000 units x £50 = £800,000.

calculating the margin of safety

The margin of safety can be calculated in units, revenue and as a percentage:

■ **units:**　　　　20,000 units – 16,000 units　　　　= 4,000 units

■ **revenue:**　　(20,000 units x £50) - £800,000　　= £200,000 revenue

■ **percentage:**　(4,000 units ÷ 20,000 units) x 100 = 20%

This means that the budgeted output could fall by 4,000 units (which equal £200,000 revenue) or 20% of budgeted output before losses will be incurred.

calculating a target profit

A target profit set at £90,000 would require sales of:

■ **units:**　　　　(£240,000 + £90,000) ÷ £15　= 22,000 units, or

■ **revenue:**　　(£240,000 + £90,000) ÷ 0.3　= £1,100,000 (the equivalent)

break-even illustrated on a graph

The break-even graph shown below uses the data and calculations from the worked example, and illustrates the features explained.

A full explanation is set out on the next page.

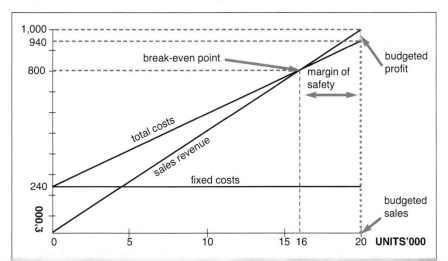

key to the break-even graph

■ The **sales revenue line** runs from the zero point (where zero units are sold and revenue is zero) to the budgeted profit where budgeted sales of 20,000 units produces £1,000,000 sales revenue.

■ The **fixed cost line** represents costs of £240,000 at all numbers of units.

■ The **total cost line** runs from where zero units = £240,000 cost (left-hand axis) to budgeted profit (right-hand side) where 20,000 units = £940,000 total cost.

   This budgeted total cost of £940,000 is made up of £240,000 fixed cost + £700,000 variable cost (ie 20,000 units x £35).

■ The **break-even point** is where the sales revenue line crosses the total cost line (ie where sales revenue = total cost). This point is at 16,000 units and £800,000 sales revenue.

■ The budgeted profit of £60,000 (ie £1,000,000 – £940,000) is shown by the vertical difference between the sales revenue line and the total cost line at 20,000 units.

■ The margin of safety of 4,000 units (£200,000 sales revenue) is shown by the distance between the break-even point (sales of 16,000 units) and the budgeted figures in units and sales revenue (sales of 20,000 units).

17 Limiting factors

WHAT IS A LIMITING FACTOR?

A limiting factor is a shortage of resources (eg materials) that prevents a business from carrying out all its planned production – in other words it restricts ('limits') output.

When a business produces more than one product and is faced with a limiting factor it should allocate its resources and production to ensure that it maximises its profit from its various products.

the key steps in dealing with limiting factors

- identify the limiting factor (eg skilled labour, materials, machine hours)
- for each product use marginal costing to calculate the **contribution per unit of limiting factor** (eg contribution per kg of material)
- rank the products based on this contribution per unit of limiting factor, highest first
- use up the limited resources by making as many units as can be sold, starting with the highest ranking product and working down to the lowest ranking product

EXAMPLE – data for a limiting factor calculation

A company makes three different products all of which require differing quantities of the same material and labour. The budget for next month is as follows:

Product	Uno	Duo	Topo	Total
Sales units	10,000	12,000	5,000	27,000
	£	£	£	£
Revenue	50,000	84,000	55,000	
less variable costs:				
Direct materials	20,000	30,000	5,000	
Direct labour	15,000	24,000	30,000	
Contribution	15,000	30,000	20,000	65,000
Fixed costs:				
Overheads				50,000
Profit				15,000
Material required:	10,000kg	15,000kg	2,500kg	27,500kg

The company has now learned that only 25,000 kg of material will be available this month.

EXAMPLE – a limiting factor calculation

To produce all the units of production in the budget the business requires 27,500kg of material but is limited to 25,000kg.

You need to calculate the contribution per kilogram of material for each product:

	Uno	Duo	Topo
Total contribution ÷ total material needed:	£15,000	£30,000	£20,000
	10,000 kg	15,000 kg	2,500 kg
Contribution per kilogram of material:	£1.50	£2.00	£8.00
Ranking of the three products by contribution per kg	3	2	1

Conclusion: use the limited material available to make as many Topos as can be sold, then Duos, and then Unos, until all the material is used up.

The next stage after establishing the priority of the production of Uno, Duo and Topo is to calculate the actual usage of the material and to draw up a revised budget.

Usage of material is as follows (see next page):

- 5,000 Topos will use 2,500kg + 12,000 Duos will use 15,000kg = 17,500 kg, which leaves 7,500kg (ie 25,000kg − 17,500kg) to make Unos.

- Each Uno uses 1 kg of material (based on the budget of 10,000 kg ÷ 10,000 units). So there is only enough material left to make and sell 7,500 Unos.

The revised budget is shown below. This maximises the contribution and therefore the profit that can be made from the limited material available.

Product	Uno	Duo	Topo	Total
Sales units	7,500	12,000	5,000	24,500
	£	£	£	£
Revenue	37,500	84,000	55,000	
Variable costs:				
Direct materials	15,000	30,000	5,000	
Direct labour	11,250	24,000	30,000	
Contribution	11,250	30,000	20,000	61,250
Fixed costs:				
Overheads				50,000
Profit				11,250

18 Special order pricing

HOW LOW CAN WE GO?

Sometimes extra sales can be generated by selling goods or services to customers who would not buy at the usual prices. The price for special orders can be lower than the normal price, provided it exceeds the marginal cost. In these circumstances 'any contribution is better than no contribution'.

It is important that lowering the price to obtain additional sales does not reduce the demand for goods at the normal prices. Sometimes the special price order may come from a market that the business does not normally sell to – for example overseas.

Lowering prices for some customers is also common in the hotel business where cheap late booking prices avoid leaving rooms empty. Provided these cheap prices exceed the marginal (variable) costs, and do not reduce the level of sales at normal prices, then the strategy will be worthwhile.

A company manufactures the 'Titan' product, with unit costs as follows:

	£
Direct materials	12
Direct labour	15
Fixed production overheads	23
Total absorption cost	50

The normal selling price is £70 per unit, and UK sales of 5,000 units are made per year at this price. The company has capacity to make and sell 6,000 units.

It has been ascertained that direct costs behave as variable costs.

A new overseas customer has offered to buy either 200 units per year for £45 each, or 800 units per year for £35 each.

The additional contribution would be either:

200 units x (£45 – (£12 + £15)) = £3,600, or

800 units x (£35 – (£12 + £15)) = £6,400

The order for 800 units at £35 would therefore increase profit by the greatest amount (£6,400) and should therefore be accepted.

19 Capital investment appraisal

THE VALUE OF MONEY IN RELATION TO TIME

Capital investment appraisal is part of the long-term decision making process of an organisation.

There are a number of techniques that can be used and most of them involve the concept that money has a 'time value'. Money is seen to be more valuable when received sooner and to cost less if paid later. This is because of the effect of interest.

Capital investment appraisal is used to decide whether it is worth investing a sum of money now – eg to buy machinery – which will generate additional cash income in the future.

All investment appraisal techniques analyse cash flows and ignore non-cash items like depreciation. The key techniques (which are explained in the next few pages) are:

■ **payback**: a simple method which works out how long it takes to get the investment back

■ **net present value** (or 'net present cost') which uses **discounted cash flow (DCF)** to take account of the time-value of money and to appraise investment projects

■ **internal rate of return**: the discount rate that produces a zero net present value

payback

This method simply involves adding up the cash that will be generated in the future by a project to work out how long it will take to pay back the amount originally invested. This calculation may involve a calculation in months as well as in years, as seen below.

> ### EXAMPLE – payback calculation
>
> A project is being considered that involves an initial investment of £55,000. The project is then expected to generate the following net cash inflows over 5 years:
>
> | Year 1 | £15,000 |
> |--------|---------|
> | Year 2 | £25,000 |
> | Year 3 | £20,000 |
> | Year 4 | £20,000 |
> | Year 5 | £20,000 |
>
> After 2 years the project will have generated £40,000 and after 3 years £60,000. We then need to calculate how many months into the third year the project will have fully repaid the investment of £55,000. The formula and calculation are:
>
> *(the remaining amount needed to reach payback point ÷ cash inflow in year 3) x 12*
>
> ((£55,000 – £40,000) ÷ £20,000) x 12 = 9 months
>
> So the investment is fully covered ('payback' is achieved) in 2 years 9 months.

discounted cash flow (DCF) and net present value (NPV)

■ This technique uses **present value (PV)** factors to calculate the present value of future cash flows.

■ The pv factors used will depend on the discount rate used and the timing of the cash flows.

■ Cash flows occurring at the present time (eg the initial investment) do not need to be discounted.

■ When all the future cash flows of a project have been discounted to their present value they can be added together.

■ If the total present value of cash flows is **positive** it is known as the '**net present value**' and is a measure of the benefit of the investment in the project.

■ If the total present value of cash flows is **negative** it is known as a '**net present cost**' and is a measure of the cost of the project.

On the next two pages are worked examples of net present cost and net present value calculations. The first shows the calculation of net present value and the second shows net present cost. The first example uses the data from the previous page.

EXAMPLE – discounted cash flow (DCF) and net present value

A company is considering a project that involves an initial investment of £55,000 and net cash inflows over a period of 5 years. The cost of capital is 10%.

	Cash flow £	PV factor @ 10%	Present value £
Year 0	-55,000	1.0000	-55,000
Year 1	15,000	0.9091	13,637
Year 2	25,000	0.8264	20,660
Year 3	20,000	0.7513	15,026
Year 4	20,000	0.6830	13,660
Year 5	20,000	0.6209	12,418
Net present value			20,401

Since the present value of the cash inflows exceeds the outflow by £20,401 this project would satisfy a company criterion of a positive NPV at 10%.

EXAMPLE – discounted cash flow (DCF) and net present cost

A company needs to decide whether to buy or to lease a delivery van. The van will be held for a period of 5 years. The financial details are as follows:

- To **buy** the van will cost £29,000. Maintenance costs are £500 per year, payable at the end of each year. The van will have no value at the end of the 5 years.
- A **lease** will require 5 annual payments of £8,000 each (including maintenance), the first amount payable immediately. The van will have no value at the end of the 5 years.
- The company's cost of capital is 10%.

	Buy				**Lease**	
	PV factor	Cash flow £	PV £		Cash flow £	PV £
Year 0	1.0000	-29,000	-29,000	Year 0	-8,000	-8,000
Year 1	0.9091	-500	-455	Year 1	-8,000	-7,273
Year 2	0.8264	-500	-413	Year 2	-8,000	-6,611
Year 3	0.7513	-500	-376	Year 3	-8,000	-6,010
Year 4	0.6830	-500	-342	Year 4	-8,000	-5,464
Year 5	0.6209	-500	-310	Year 5	0	0
Net present cost			-30,896	Net present cost		-33,358

The lower net present cost will result if the van is purchased (- £30,896) rather than leased (- £33,352) and so purchasing the van will be the preferred option.

internal rate of return (IRR)

- The interest rate that provides a **net present value of zero** when applied to a project is known as the **internal rate of return (IRR)** of the project.

- The higher the IRR, the more financially advantageous the project.

- Organisations wishing to invest will set a specific IRR that potential investments must achieve. It is likely that this IRR will reflect the organisation's cost of capital.

In the worked example that follows a number of internal rates of return are illustrated.

EXAMPLE – internal rate of return (IRR)

In practice a business would normally use a spreadsheet function to calculate the IRR of a project, as the formulas involved are very complex.

The net present value (NPV) in the previous example (see page 109) is £20,401 using a discount rate of 10%.

The table below gives the NPVs of the same project using several different discount rates.

---

internal rate of return comparisons

Discount rate	Present Value of Cash inflows	Investment	NPV
	£	£	£
8%	79,511	-55,000	24,511
10%	75,385	-55,000	20,401
15%	66,476	-55,000	11,476
20%	59,118	-55,000	4,118
25%	52,986	-55,000	-2,014

zero NPV

From this information you can see that the NPV of the project will be zero when the discount rate is between 20% and 25%. A good estimate would be 22.5%.

The actual IRR of this project is 23.26%.

an organisation's criteria for dealing with investment appraisal

An organisation is likely to have its own criteria for approving capital investment.

The organisation may set required levels for one or more of the following investment appraisal techniques, for example:

- ▓ payback within a certain period of time, for example 3 years

- ▓ a positive net present value when a specified pv factor is used (eg 10%)

- ▓ a minimum internal rate of return, for example an IRR of 15% or more

Discounted cash flow can also be used to compare alternative projects that are necessary but will always constitute a cost – for example deciding whether to buy or rent delivery vehicles. In this case the same principles are used to calculate the present value of the future cash flows and the lowest net present cost could be used as a company criterion.

20 Memory aids

KEEPING YOUR MEMORY FIT

The human brain is an odd organ – you can remember the most useless facts, but when it comes to complex matters such as accounting procedures the mind can go completely blank. But it is possible to train your brain.

At the beginning of this Guide there are some revision tips which suggest that you can study effectively and recall information by . . .

■ **Observing**, *ie remembering what information looks like on the page, using diagrams, lists, mind-maps and colour coding. Memory is very visual.*

■ **Writing** *information down, using flash cards, post-it notes, notes on a phone. It is the actual process of writing which helps to fix the information in the brain.*

■ **Learning** *by regularly going through your course notes and text books. Find a 'study buddy' in your class (or online) to teach and test each other as the course progresses.*

■ **Chill out** when you get tired. Give your brain a chance to recover. Get some exercise and fresh air, work out. In the ancient world there was the saying that a fit body was usually home to a fit mind.

■ **Treats** – promise yourself rewards when you have finished studying – meet friends, eat chocolate, have a drink, listen to music.

exam preparation

■ **Practice, practice, practice** when preparing for your assessment.

Practice the questions and assessments in the Osborne Books workbooks.

Practice the free online assessments on the Osborne Books website:

Log on to www.osbornebooks.co.uk/elearning

using the memory aids

On the next few pages are blank spaces for you to set out ways of remembering many of the definitions and formulas needed for your AAT assessment.

managing materials inventory

Enter in the blank spaces definitions of the terms in the left-hand column.

inventory buffer	
lead time	
re-order level	
re-order quantity	

costing methods

Enter in the blank spaces examples of organisations which are likely to use the costing methods listed on the left.

unit costing	
job costing	
batch costing	
service costing	
process costing	

cost apportionment

Enter in each of the blank spaces appropriate ways to apportion between responsibility centres the indirect costs listed on the left.

factory rent	
depreciation of machinery	
power for machinery	
factory heating	
canteen costs	

break-even analysis

Enter in each of the blank spaces the formulas for the terms listed on the left.

contribution	
contribution/sales ratio	
break-even (units)	
margin of safety (units)	
margin of safety (% of budgeted sales)	

index